The Double House of Life

Also by Randy Blasing

LIGHT YEARS
TO CONTINUE
THE PARTICLES

THE DOUBLE HOUSE OF LIFE

To Al,

with long-standing admiration —

Poems by
Randy Blasing

[signature]

1989

Persea Books / New York

Some of these poems originally appeared in *The Literary Review, Michigan Quarterly Review,* and *Poetry* ("North End," "Pirated Version," "Kingdom Come," "An Album Family," "Richfield," "Refuge," "Golden Valley," "Divining Rod," "Calling," "Within Limits," "Triptych," and "White Bread," copyright © 1985, 1986, 1987, 1989 by the Modern Poetry Association).

For information, please write to the publisher:

Persea Books, Inc.
60 Madison Avenue
New York, New York 10010

Library of Congress Cataloging-in-Publication Data

Blasing, Randy.
  The double house of life : poems / Randy Blasing.
    p.   cm.
  ISBN 0-89255-143-7 : $9.95
  I. Title.
PS3552.L38D6   1989
811'.54—dc19   89-2973
                                                                   CIP

Set in Bembo by Keystrokes, Lenox, Massachusetts.
Manufactured in the United States of America.

First Edition

for Mutlu

CONTENTS

I

AN ALBUM FAMILY

1
A good-time Charlie from the start, my father
wasn't even a year when he got caught
laughing at the whole idea of being
here: the black hole
of his mouth swallows the light whitening
his baby bonnet, circa 1912.

The *o* his lips have formed
is shaded like a zero on an early
printout, dark as the light-starved snow-draped earth
sledgehammered open to the sun
fifty-two years later at Fort Snelling
or as these letters, my own charred remains.

2
Last night I'd shaved my beard to play the baby-
faced infant I am there
in the black-&-white photograph of me
cheek to cheek with my mother, lips twisted
into a faint smile as if I'm just learning

to kiss. Her eyes
look faraway, as though she can't believe
what's happened. She stretched out her arms & cried
in my dream, imploring me one more time
to bring her back to life. It seems the flowers

climbing all over her like shadows spring
from the leafy vines covering her chair
& papering the living room,
the way I am growing out of her hands.

PIRATED VERSION

Lost as usual in the shallow depths
of the pond-green aquarium
where wide-eyed guppies nose around a little
man in a diving suit beside
a minute treasure chest, the light from above

seemingly frozen & the only sound
water bubbling through the filter, I stand
to add a gold star to my name again
today by being a good boy & not
crying out for a shot of Novocain.

My mother has walked me here through the snow
—up the street, down the hill, & past
Lake Nokomis—to let Dr. Elasky
fill more of the twenty-seven
cavities he's found in my baby teeth

before I'm even five. Inside,
above the chair, he's hung these model airplanes
(a yellow Piper Cub my favorite)
from the ceiling to keep my mind
off the business at hand, but pain

always blocks them out & leaves me conscious
of nothing save his pencil-line black mustache,
plus my mother trying to quiet me
with the words, "Oh, Randy, you know
it doesn't hurt

that much." I don't know anything
yet, at least not the way knowing

just means sitting still for something
everyone says
is for the best but I feel in my bones

to be the opposite. Like a frogman
undermining a ship, I stay in the dark
below the surface & the distant static
of voices with their foreign words, seeing
by my own lights, knowing what I know.

VOWELS

Flushed out from under the mahogany
dining table where I played with my cars
among its spider legs & heard my mother
save me from the thunder
one evening with the story they were bowling
in the sky, I was first assigned a bus
with a number too big for my small mind
& then taken away from home a distance
I could cover but never would have walked
only to find myself

in school. Once at my desk, I stared at where
the inkwell dating from my parents' day
had been, a black-stained knothole no larger
than the pitch-dark o's my father showed me
keyhole saws cut in pole houses designed
for sudden Y-tailed soaring purple martins.
I was so terrified
of raising my hand & asking permission
to leave my seat I wet my pants
instead, but gradually I put

two & two together: certain
letters of the alphabet were different
because they breathed life into it, like holes
I punched in the blue-&-white lid I kept
on every many-footed caterpillar
I locked up behind glass to watch grow wings,
& let me breathe out words as I sat buried
in my reader, pronouncing Dick & Jane
alive who saw Spot run &, walled in
by windows, flying with him through the pages.

RICHFIELD

The smoldering odor
of dead leaves raked against my stone foundation
tells me it's 1950 & I'm fishing
cool salamanders out

of a window well. Charcoal-black
with splotches of flesh-pink,
they look like they've survived the third-degree
burns featured in my father's *Life*

at War. That summer my uncle dropped down
on all fours in the yard, the grown-from-seed
lawn glossy as Easter
grass, & trapped a rabbit

under his hat, I wanted to keep it
out back in a cage I awoke
the next sun-shot morning to find
smeared with guts: a cat. The scene of the crime

marked the spot where a robin froze
so a kid given a Red Ryder gun
for his birthday could squeeze a gold BB
into its thumb-size head. When I confessed,

the word got chanted through the bulldozed farm
country by the Turnbull boys, whose father
I watched a court of law railroad for shooting
the dog harassing his pet fox. His eldest,

a tattooed green Marine, coasted me up
& down the block on his Harley-Davidson
one warm evening after supper, before
going to Korea. Then came the night

I didn't think I'd live
to see the day—tomorrow—I'd turn seven:
my candle-lit family of three
hugged the southwest corner

of the basement & waited for the white
lightning to nail the oak outside our door
before the wind funneled our house
into the sky. Later I saw

refrigerators lying on their sides
in the mud, too big & fat to get back
on their feet without help, & snapped
power lines crisscrossed the newly paved streets

like black snakes sunning themselves in the mild
aftermath. I went on living
in the breathing spaces
between the lines the growing suburb drew

around me, & today I turn
over this ground to find
the straight & narrow shade-dark rows
seeded with light.

THE ONLY CHILD

Before bed, I weathered the cold & saw
the snow crystallizing the yard
sparkle under the January moon
like the white quartz shot with fool's gold

I discovered in the Black Hills
when I was nine, its glitter faint
as minor stars or the tiny diamonds
the sun pinpoints in granite & fresh asphalt.

The woodsmoke in the air
smelled like the Prince Albert burning
in my grandfather's pipe again
after thirty years. He was still talking

about leaving Wales to fight for Queen
Victoria in the Orange Free State, the words
alone so magical they made a place
in me for good. Then I thought how

I'd always listen to my grandmother
in horror when she'd tell about the single
orange she got for Christmas back in Norway
a century ago. At night I dreamed

I found myself standing
on a steep cliff & gazing at the navy
Mediterranean below. Elated,
I watched it turn so deep a blue the scene

blacked out before my eyes, & I awoke
to total night, knowing
where I stood finally: I was the end
of the story, the screen gone dark, the sea

erased, the reason the words had to be
repeated enough times
for me to love them before I could say what
they meant, the story told once & for all.

DOUBLE LIFE

I used to live
for Sunday, when the funny papers came
in color. All week long
the world was black & white, from the landscape
our picture window framed—snow (it was always
winter) spiked with wrought-iron
trees—to the choice of drinks
at the table: coffee
(plain) for the grown-ups & icy
milk for us kids. But Sundays brought me Dick
Tracy's crazy yellow hat, not to mention
his freckled sidekick Sam's
purple bowtie & green sports
jacket. No one I knew went around dressed
like them, but I never thought twice
about it. What mattered
was the whole idea of being free
to play with shades
of meaning, like a child
fiddling with the dials
of a color TV when nobody
is watching. I was eight,
& I had learned to read
after it hit me halfway through first grade
my world had gone to pieces (twenty-six,
to be exact). One day
I raised my head to find them all lined up—
the "big" letters above the "small"—& marching
around the schoolroom, chalked
on a narrow frieze-like band of blackboard
nailed to the walls. Still, I asked my father
to read me the funnies those movie-bright
mornings before we joined a church, & after

we'd wrestle in the living room. Each time
our roughhousing ended with him
pinning me to the floor,
where I'd lie paralyzed
as if in an iron lung & stop breathing
under his weight. The next day he would go
& disappear for one more week—
"on the road," we called it. While he was gone,
my mother & I walked
everywhere, & she took my mind
off the perpetual sub-zero weather
by pointing out that I could see
my breath, which clued me in
to the spiritual dimension
of things & showed me to keep my eyes open
for the invisible. If, as she kept
saying, life was what I made it,
I'd have to breathe
life into things, colored as they would be
by my view of them. Soon I began hunching
over a globe & studying its colors,
in my own world at last. Little did I know
our words paint the earth according
to our lights, until the world has its own
story to tell, pieced together
from each of ours, like that stained-glass
chapel in Paris where the sun
illuminates the various Bible stories
going around the room. I picture myself
smoking like a chimney
in the cold, walking through the snow
like a character in a comic strip
still on the drawing board, the cloud
of hot air ballooning from my mouth empty
yet expressive of my secret desire
to breathe a word.

KINGDOM COME

I held my breath
waiting for spring: the rising undercurrent
of melted snow taking the street
by storm, & the sun no longer
someone's idea of a joke but something
capable of bringing down the palace
of ice the cold had raised by working night
& day for what had seemed
an eternity. Meanwhile, people said
I had my whole life ahead of me,
& I believed them. Early
mornings my mother whispered in my ear
to wake up, I stumbled through the motions
of preparing myself
for school & heard her busy in the kitchen.
As if still dreaming, I'd sit
down then as now
to my half of a pink grapefruit
dusted with sugar, which gave it the kind
of rosy glow the snow took on
once the mahogany dark outside
had gone up in smoke & before the sallow
light of day broke
the gloom like the headlights
of the black-numbered pumpkin school bus
lumbering down the road to stop for me,
its brakes squeaking the way, at every step,
the frozen ground would creak
like the hall floor at home
under the ugly, buckled-up
black galoshes I couldn't wait
to deposit in the cloakroom,

my last name neatly printed in blue ink
on a tiny white adhesive strip
inside each one. I lived
for the future so long the present got
to be a dream, a dress
rehearsal for a play not meant to be
performed, & only tomorrow
was real. In time I wrote
off today & imagined myself living
in the world to come. Just as I always kept
my Johnny Pesky fielder's glove
well lubricated with neat's-foot
oil all winter, I nursed my desire for spring
& learned to lay up treasure, in my words,
against a day I had no hope of seeing.

FLYING LESSON

Leaving my mother sleeping in the dark
Sunday mornings, my father & I drove out
to Flying Cloud. I fell asleep again

while he logged hours in a V-tailed gold
Bonanza, always waking me in time
to let me take the stick & lower us

to earth. The summer I was ten, we shadowed
the Minnesota River in a silver
Aerocoupe, the black X

of our plane marking the spots all along
the pea-green valley where he'd grown like corn.
As we followed the course the river charted

for us, the wind kindly
bared my father's head for him when he bowed
over the water, his white cap

surrendered to the air the way ten years
later he'd die to have his ashes scattered
above the holy ground he rose up from,

& I never took my eyes off the land
under us, just as I would root myself
in words I found that carried me away.

WHITE BREAD

One morning I woke to apricot light
out my bedroom window in the still-vacant
lot not yet forested
with orange two-by-fours—another house
rising between us & the corner place,
where I first tasted tangerines the people
there had got from California
& dipped (if memory serves) in sugar section
by golden section. My white pj's
were neatly decorated with cowboys
riding tiny bucking broncos,
& I'd hallucinated the motif
on my papered four walls, delirious once
with measles. I remember my grandfather
eased me back asleep, as he had soothed
my mother as a girl with scarlet fever.
When I felt better, she would read to me
about the Little Green Car, & I'd listen
to the Lone Ranger on the radio
at night. In the kitchen
I found my mother working at the table
she'd painted red
herself, her square bread board floured white.
Outside on the line, my father's white shirts
she always called the size of tents while standing
at her ironing board snapped in the breeze
like flags, & the starchy smell in the air
went to my head like pop fizz up my nose.
Filled out with wind, they blew up big as clouds
& sprinkled me with rain that gave me shivers
as they dried in the sun. The light was still
everything I could have wanted, but then
I couldn't trust the sun
to be there for me every day.

Just to get out of bed, I needed something
to anticipate before the sun set
on me, as if each day were my birthday
& I could look forward to an ivory
plastic guitar with ebony trim small
as a ukulele, two-tone
(black & white) cowboy boots, plus a silver-
studded black leather holster set with twin
pearly handled six-guns blond Hopalong
Cassidy made popular Saturday
mornings he fought the snow
on our first TV. Day in & day out
I came up with whatever lit a fire
under me each morning, & I harbored
what the light promised
like a secret. Setting my heart
on this or that meant I was never bored
at least, because I knew
the little thing I envisioned the day
held out was waiting. When I stopped being
satisfied with such small crumbs as my life
doled out to me
to savor, I began to put my faith
in divining the magic words
that would align the world
& my desire to be at one
with it, however briefly & in theory
only. My wish to speak
without speaking became a daily lump
in my throat, an ever-present
feeling of words about to come
to me so that I'd meet the light
on equal terms by rendering the same
in my image, the way the minuscule
shadows memory traces day by day
tell the other side of the sun's story.

GOLDEN VALLEY

My first night there I couldn't sleep
from all the goldenrod I'd sniffed
playing war until it got dark

in the still-wild valley below our house,
where the Soo Line ran tanks to South Korea
those days my father stood to be called back

to active duty. My mother meanwhile
needled him about using every last
four-letter word in the book when he talked

to the home office. Swearing not to let
business become my life, I vowed to make
life my business, if on paper only.

Caterpillars had leveled Noble Grove
for our development, but across the tracks
the woods—beeches, maples, oaks—remained standing.

Later, when they were stripped of green & gold
& snow fell as if for good, the charred trees
our picture window displayed like a page

of upright characters showed me
how to absorb the losses mounting daily,
the red ink in our blood, & come

out burnt yet in the black
someday, letter-perfect
when everything was said & done.

II

METAMORPHOSES AT CANNON POINT

for Mutlu

1
Bees, gold flecks suspended
in morning light, attack a solitary

wild olive frilly in the breeze,
its pea-sized fruit bunched together like grapes.

Somewhere in the shade, a cicada turned
on by the sun

buzzes away, humming
like a power line in a wind.

A sparrow masked as a handful of dust
loses rust skullcap, dove-gray chest, & gold

epaulets in the leaves, then hops
up & down on a branch

as if inspired to take flight
while, so to speak, singing.

2
Watching for snakes, I blaze a trail
across a field swarming with purple flowers:

thyme. Two red poppies May forgot
survive, lip to bleeding lip, into mid-

July. The sun, now outlining in black
the cell-shaped lozenges of white stones beached

below the headland, has its eye on us.
When I look back for you, you've dropped from sight

& gone over the edge
for all I know, leaving me alone

with the death rattle of the surf
shooting dice on the stony shore.

3
As day bleeds into night, the sky
opens up: a barrage

of lasers city lights
kept us from seeing

coming, the stars
pin us down on the earth, crickets

picking up the katydids' beat
like a too-rapid pulse.

4
The yeasty salt-smell of bread fresh each morning
rises from the blond cutting board,

as slice after honey-gold slice falls our way
like light given us day by day.

5
Cicadas click
incessantly:

backgammon dice
in a coffeehouse.

6
A sickle moon
scarlet as if

dripping blood
cuts through the west.

7
Like ringing in my ears—too many greenish
pink-to-mauve salt-cured breakfast olives upping

my blood pressure?—the so-called August bugs
electrify the air this July morning,

the sea at my feet midnight-blue,
a wind-inflamed olive tree sparking white

overhead. The sun strikes
again, a day-long lightning bolt.

8
An omen out of Homer I can read:
three black birds flying on my left hand

& me flat on my back
in his Aegean, morning-glory blue

on the surface but at bottom dark green
as graveyard cypresses.

9
Each afternoon the sea burns phosphorous
along the line dividing it

from the Greek island offshore, thus
italicizing the foreign horizon.

At dusk its not-so-distant lights
begin to glimmer like a swarm

of lightning bugs—shades of the firefly stars
that nightly punctuate another day.

10
All days are different, all the same,
like the gold bars

of our daily bread the faithful
baker leaves stacked

up & waiting for us
a morning at a time.

11
A plum-blue, green-walnut-emerald, clay-gold
prayer rug glows

like a stained-glass window
with earth's own light.

12
Moving in waves
in the wind tonight, a lone olive foams

like the sea, its fish-silver leaves
whitecaps under the moon.

13
Last night's wind has died, & the smoke-blue sea
flat-out seethes this morning, as work continues

on my neighbor's stone wall. *Dawn* comes in color
without fail: a gunned-down diplomat bleeds

under newspapers on today's front page,
while on the back a sun-loving tourist

goes naked save a boldfaced hyphen through
each nipple &, between her legs, one fat

black asterisk. Things will heat up
until, next door, the day

laborer still a boy
buttons on his blue shirt

once more, slicks back
his watered-down hair, & calls it a day.

14
The full moon pans the sky's
black-flowing stream

for gold nuggets
of stars.

15
In the cobweb-silver
sky before dawn,

Venus dangles
like a dew-bright spider.

16
The carpenter's brother, a stonemason
of sorts, never goes anywhere

without the tweed cap with a little visor
he wears at such an angle that a shadow

always veils his face, & today he comes
bearing a gift

stolen from his brother-in-law: a round
sunflower-gold melon downy

—I discover lightly
cupping it in one hand—with all

but invisible blond fuzz like an aura
in the sun, the kind women here

carry two at a time
in front of them, breast-high.

17
The sea shadows the wind
& registers

its every move
like a blue flame.

18
Before the moth-eaten moon turns up, bats
harvest mosquitoes in the air above

a casaba patch, the sporadic stars
melon seeds planted in black earth.

19
Time & again
the rising sun

bloodies the sea
like the end of the world.

20
On the rocks, head buried
in my hands, I can't bring myself to look

toward the low roar in the air. You come
running up the shore to tell me

what I just missed: a big white fish-shaped jet
with no wings gone

in a flash! I freeze, waiting
for it to hit.

21
Wiped out by the sun, people straggle back
from the beach like survivors of a shipwreck:

dazed, half naked, clutching what few
belongings they have left.

22
Blackening some of us like walking shadows,
bronzing others to look

like frozen gods, the sun
reduces for a day

even dung in a field
to gold.

23
Divine July is history now, August
half evaporated, & the first clouds

in a month-long string of flawless
star-sapphire days

cast a shadow dark as the days to come
over the sea.

24
The nightly blackout shows the sky
spotted with stars thick as scales on a fish.

The Milky Way drifts through the dark
like smoke from the future.

25
Noon sun off the water too bright
to contemplate, the boatman relaxes

with a comic book, no takers so far
for his three red-&-white rowboats that say

"For Rent" where they should have names. Meanwhile, light
obscures the other shore.

26
In the wake of a small, candy-striped trawler
scooting home with the day's catch, gulls

speckle the blue water
like ashes scattered on the sea.

27
Staring down the gold-dusty black abyss
of the night sky, I catch myself

plummeting forever
into the earth.

28
Wind blows the blue sea green
today & tosses up

waves crested white like endless rows
of headstones in a field.

29
Like sacrificial lambs,
fleecy waves beat a path

across the rolling green
to their end on the beach.

30
In broad daylight
a diver softens up

the coral octopus he's brought
back from the underworld,

lashing the rocks with it
as if it were a scourge.

31
Watching a peach of a sun slip
through the mountains' fingers

moves you to say you love this place,
here but a day.

32
The pearl-milky, pond-flat, late-August sea
previews the days I'll miss

seeing, gone come
September when the words

on everyone's lips will be "like a sheet,"
meaning the water, & the air will be

breathless every single day, as if summer
hung by a thread.

33
Swimming out of the depths, you rise
from the foam at sea's edge

into the sun, your quicksilver presence
dripping with light.

34
Evening wind sends shivers
through an olive tree

with a hissing sound
as of wood catching fire.

35
Walking the plank of a finite
number of days

remaining, I open my eyes
wider by the minute.

36
To live you have to give yourself to what
you see, & see

the light: a tawny mare's flank & her tan
foal's mane gilded by the soon-to-set sun.

37
Paradise, to behold the light
in any shape

any given day: thistles, yet,
have hearts of gold.

38
Each day more precious than the one
before: this light

that turns everything gold
is all there is.

39
The tonic air lifting
my spirits like nothing,

all I ask is to keep
walking with you

side by side in the light,
each other's shadow to the end.

40
Out of nowhere
here at the last,

a minute finch
lights a second

on an olive branch, flares
solid gold in the sun,

& high-tails it
into thin air.

III

THE LUMINIST

Is the silver
mirroring the clouds a river
or a pond? The trees, mere charcoal

shadows of themselves, deepen the gloom
of the time (late fall) & place (New
England, if those patchy gray areas

are rocks). Yet from a distance
the total picture grows
luminous, for reasons

a closer look beyond the glass
wavy with age
makes clear: you spot flashes

of color—a thicket of mauve, leaves
lichen-like smudges of mustard-yellow—
& find the pearl glow in the air

arises from an ivory line
crossing the water, which the inky shores
illuminate by contrast. Good as gold

because in short supply, the light is worth
in the end only as much as the paper
it's printed on.

NORTH END

1. JANUARY COUNTRY

Crows rule the roost, black as the ice
glazing a no-name pond
at the point the spring continues

feeding into it. Snow
whites out even the trees, sticking
to their trunks like the paint some old wives' tale

says scares off gypsy moths. My thoughts
take a turn for the worse, & I recall
the day that did this, all those people going

*As I live & die, the sky has a mind
to bury us!* Flakes thick as stars on the flag
settled like ashes on the smoking houses . . .

Only now something clicks
in my head like the cold turnstile
of another season locking

behind me. *Where to from here?* The way
the freezing air drives the carp in the pond
deeper into their element, the stillness

turns me to words. Crows punctuate the white
like periods that sentence me
to what I've said.

2. GRAY MATTER

Overnight, March
invades January,
& the ice starts to break

in its wake. Mist lifts off the gray river
like dreams evaporating in the light,
like the spirit of the water rising

as a ghost to hover
above it—proof
the invisible lives.

All day, in one corner
of my mind, the vision builds up
like the pearl of the sky.

3. FEBRUARY ANNIVERSARY

Bare forked maples blacken in winter rain
as if possessed by their shadows,
like mourners all gathered around a grave

in silence. Fog clouds my view
of a white lake
through the trees: it's a scene

straight out of a misty Japanese scroll
painting of a moment of change
frozen in time to remind me

of loss. Yet the harder
I have to look, the more clearly
I see. Peering

into the distance of the other shore,
I drift off across the water
to condense myself, like ink on a page.

DIVINING ROD

Winters I practiced swinging my Al Kaline
Louisville Slugger in the living room
mirror, trying to keep a level bat
whether the pitcher in my mind

threw down & out or up & in. When summer
after summer saw me look good
striking out every chance I got, I traded
my lumber for a Venus No. 2.

In hopes of making contact & a name
for myself after all, I grooved my strokes
across each page, delineating features
I dreamed were mine. At first I couldn't draw

from memory, which I wrote off as pure
imagination then but now follow
to the end, a blind man
trusting where my stick leads.

TRIPTYCH

1. LAST SPRING

I stuck my nose into a hornet's nest
of blossoming wisteria, & the scent
presented me with Fleer's
sugar-coated baseball-card gum my mother
bought me in quest
of my heroes each time she stopped
at Noble Drug for L&M's
some thirty years ago. Late in the day

I called her up
in Florida & heard she'd had more trouble
breathing. When I lied the sun-blackened lilacs
here were still holding on, she turned
the clock back sixty years & smelled the white
lilacs at home one last time in my words.

2. EARTHBOUND

My father used an alias
while still in high school to play semi-pro
baseball on Sunday so that his God-fearing
parents, who didn't smoke

or drink or even read the funny papers
on the Sabbath, wouldn't see his name Monday
morning in the box score & know he'd broken
one more commandment carved in stone.

In the future, when he mowed the grass, say,
in lieu of church, he always swore

the better the day, the better the deed—
even to the minister's face.

His sole hope of any life after death
coming to him rested on his stories
I'd taken to heart, hallowing his name
by worshiping the sun in so many words.

3. PATCHWORK

All I heard growing up were biases
& selvages, both as mysterious
to me today as they were then. Her black
& silver pinking shears squeaking away,
my mother made her own clothes from the fabrics
out of New York my father sold in widely
scattered Dakota towns from his home base
in Minneapolis. Received opinion
back in the Fifties said that blue & green
didn't mix, but I remember one day
the two of them agreed those colors matched
as well as pine trees & a cloud-free sky.
Their son at last, I weave my biases
together with whatever I can salvage.

CALLING

Researchers can duplicate any climate
but I will keep from them my little world,
the hothouse I grew up inside. The glass
my own breath steamed up made faces
back at me, minute clouds I breathed
into existence & endowed
with eyes & a mouth as if humanizing
a snowman's blank expression. At six,
when I emerged from my fog long enough
to see something—the alphabet—was flying
in Miss Parks's class, everyone
else had got a handle on it
& learned to exercise their liberal will
to power over words, but I was trying
to come to terms with the black marks lined up
against me in the book & then X-rayed
on the board, where black was white & vice versa.
As if following a musical score,
I had to rhyme the sounds that came
out of me & the letters with their code
of silence others took to mean they were
there to be used as tools—say by a priest
working old Mr. Stevens for his soul.
Eventually I translated my voice
to the page, just as even now my tongue
secretly shapes each word I read or write.
Since words well up inside me, I don't know
how to calculate their effect
or twist them to my ends to get whatever
leverage I desire, it may be,
at X's expense, the way certain people
will do certain things & afterwards plead

it wasn't really them—they'd merely wanted
to go from A to B by any means
at their disposal. For the life of me
I can't outline my moves
in advance any more
than I can think before opening my mouth,
so that I might not always tell the truth
but speak, for better or worse, from the heart,
as if still conversing
with my imaginary friend I dialed
on my play phone before I started school.
He or she, whose name continues
to escape me, was the same as me, only
different. I could surprise myself with what
I found to say, yet rest assured someone
listened at the other end of the line.

WITHIN LIMITS

I never learned
to follow the music, always out of step
with what was playing at each Friday hop

the way my heart, decades
down the road, skips a beat repeatedly
& counterpoints time's goose step round the clock.

To join the dance in everybody's blood,
I had to make my own music
as when, counting syllables at my desk

those nights as many years
ago, I found my ten fingers perfect
for playing variations on the beat

that pulses through the feet of a long line
of dancers who filled in the blank
with their own signatures.

GRAMMAR SCHOOL

An old school patterned on a red-brick mill
the children, following
in their parents' footsteps, filed into once
upon a time is pushing up
tulips today's pupils have grown
from unchanged green-&-orange flip-top boxes
of Crayolas & their teachers have planted
in rows in the dust-smoked
windows, discouraging
class after class from daydreaming its way
outside. Beginning in the fall
of second grade, my mother shuttled me
between her family home & Lee
Avenue Elementary, near where
our new split-level ranch was going up
in time, she said, for summer. I looked forward
to spring in Minnesota more than ever
&, like an infant piecing things together
word by word, composed my own view of it
from the four elements. Although the sun
from what I saw left much to be
desired, I started at the top
& sketched a dandelion-yellow spider
weaving an invisible web of light
across a low cloud ceiling the cream-color
of drawing paper. Earth,
the bottom line, gave rise
to nameless flowers of every stripe. Water
appeared as rain, not gray like April showers
of broken mechanical-pencil leads
I watched nail down winter's coffin
through the glass, but sky-blue dotted lines

I slanted at a forty-five degree
angle to indicate the wind
offstage, which sometimes stitched a long-tailed T-
frame kite into the upper lefthand corner
of a scene as further proof it took part
in the action. Since then it's cleared the set
of home & family, the cast
of characters all blown away except
for the stick figure anchoring the kite,
twisted & transfigured
by now into a letter among letters.

REFUGE

A stand of paper birches years & years
of lovers have tattooed with their black hearts
& initials shades the starved baby tapping
his mother's breast like a downy woodpecker.

In the marsh behind him, red-winged blackbirds
go down in flames to feed
cattail-sheltered nestlings, while bullfrogs
tune their bass instruments as if rehearsing

for the night ahead. Here, where generations
have come to leave their mark
in passing, the plus signs
still add up to something like desire:

all the letters of the alphabet
in love with each other to this day.

SQUID

I've seen Aegean men
spear squid out of the blue
to take home to their wives,
who know just what to do

with it: first, peel away
the freckled sheath of skin
from flesh creamy as rose
marble, then (as you happen

to be doing right
this minute) extract
intact the transparent
backbone, which fits between

your fingers like a pen.
Squeezing the daylights
out of the now-flaccid
creature, you watch it

blacken in your hands
like a little white lie
disappearing behind
a smoke screen of ink.

BIRTHDAY OFF CHIOS

Waves pile into the shore ad infinitum,
countless as days without a living soul
to number them, & I come like a pilgrim
at sunset to be cured
of my recurrent blue hallucination:
leeched of all color, the widow-black sky
catches me in its gleaming spider web

of stars. Tonight the wind that's bent
the olive outside my door here
double in twice my forty years
drives a wedge between me
& my inkblot shadow,
which makes its way alone
across a gulf white as a blind man's cane.

IV

STARFISH

1

Today they caught my eye, the shoals
of pyracantha berries coral-orange
in clear September light, & I remembered

coast-hugging robins will depend on them
to make it back to spring. Sunset flaring
salmon-pink now, my enlarged heart

jumps like a red mullet
when I think of the fish
swimming in your belly as of this morning.

2

A prairie child hearing the sea,
I press my ear to your belly
as to a bleached conch shell. Sounding

your depths, I am my father listening
for the life-&-death difference
between whales & Japanese submarines

forty-two years ago
on his destroyer in the South Pacific,
months before I was born. Tonight, sonar

gives shape to what waits to torpedo you:
a skull-white globe trails clouds of swirling snow
in the dark, ghostly as a colorless

TV's fluttery picture of the earth
shot from space, & I pinpoint the future
on the screen where

an infinitesimal heart
pulses like the center of a starfish,
like the eye of a hurricane on radar.

3
Out here, under the stars—
I mean, there in the night
where it's all being put

together this winter a microdot
at a time, minnow-quick & inching forward
by leaps & bounds. Ten digits to my name,

I was once my warring father's only proof
of divinity. Then my mother called
into the distance, "When it happens

to me," & I pretended not
to hear, as if still just a child
whose mother couldn't die. Up above, nothing

ever goes wrong, while down below we are
wrong from the word "go": they're nothing but
chancy, our combinations in the dark.

4
You wonder what the future will look like.
As my good aunt said at my mother's funeral,
"What else is there

but resemblance?" It unearths such relations
(family or otherwise) as teach us
the world is not carved in granite

but something we envision in the raw
material at hand & build up
invisibly inside by constantly

discovering our ever-changing place
in it, which hinges on the granddaddy
of four-letter words: *like*.

5
This evening you fit the curve of my hand
perfectly, & trying
to put my finger on what slips

out from under my thumb
like a tropical fish darting around
in an unlit aquarium, I'm small

again & feel the world
spin in my palm
back there in my grandfather's dim

extra room, playing roulette with his globe
to see its many colors break
down into worlds

that stop & linger at my finger tips
an instant at a time as if
within easy reach, like plum-colored Turkey.

Now, when I picture your infinitely finite
skin diver probing every inch
of space as if to touch bottom

in your landlocked sea, the child I was falls
asleep once more imagining
the borders of the universe.

6
A high-flying jet cutting the blue down
to size stitches east & west together
like a spider, its silk-white thread unraveling

as it goes. From his post in a bloomed cherry,
a hawk-eyed robin scrambles to fight off
a divebombing jay intent on raiding

his nest of loose ends in a neighboring
long-needled pine, where his black-headed mate
broods unflinching. Let that be you.

7
"Like waiting for the Bomb
to drop," the doctor jokes, meaning the baby
expected any day hangs over you

like a nameless descendant of Type-A
"Little Boy" born out of the blue
forty-odd years before.

8
It begins with a distant cry
like a bird's you can't believe you have heard
in the dark before dawn early in spring,

& soon the blood-shot purple face
of something, eyes
puckered shut, surfaces from its lagoon.

Flushed out of hiding, your chameleon
changes in the light: dawn-rosy fingers
turn baby shrimp, pearl toes lilies

of the valley. Day One he plays
close to the vest, clinging
to my chest like a ladybug. His head

is fuzzy like an apricot & round
as a fat McIntosh.
His eyes are blueberries.

He cries like water seething to a boil,
& he hiccups like so many
champagne corks popping New Year's Eve.

Mouth like the sweet calyx of a day lily,
little fists like peony buds, nipples
shadowy as the moon

in daylight, heart beating
like a hummingbird's wings, he dives
into your breast.

9
He eats like a bird, a downy-
headed duckling
blindly open-mouthed. He himself

is warm & buttery, like a hot loaf
of my grandmother's bread. Grandfathers nothing
but bones anymore breathe again

in his chest, lips, & cheeks. Seashells
for ears, he wrinkles up his face
like a quince, for he grows

quizzical before all things. His wizened
far-off gaze reflects the distance
he has come in nine months. His eyes

look the sky's smoky midnight-blue at dusk
today, Venus cradled
by May's crescent moon glowing with the milky

aura of its future. I wish him luck
as good as mine that he fell like a star
into my arms.